Metaphor of the
Womb

Apostle Stevie Okauru

ZONAZIN PRESS

Copyright © 2022 Stevie Okauru

All rights reserved. No part of this publication may be reproduced, distributed, or transmitted in any form or by any means, including photocopying, recording, or other electronic or mechanical methods, without the prior written permission of the publisher, except in the case of brief quotations embodied in critical reviews and certain other noncommercial uses permitted by copyright law. For permission requests, write to the publisher, addressed "Attention: Permissions Coordinator," at the address below.

Zonazin press
www.zonazin.com

Ordering Information:
Quantity sales. Special discounts are available on quantity purchases by corporations, associations, and others. For details, contact the publisher at the address above.
Orders by U.S. trade bookstores and wholesalers. Please contact Big Distribution:

visit www. oraclemiracle.org.com.

Printed in the United States of America

TABLE OF CONTENTS

CHAPTER 1 1
          THANKSGIVING, PRAISE, AND PRAYER

CHAPTER 2 11
          DEFINITION OF TERMS

CHAPTER 3 17
          METAPHORIC WOMB

CHAPTER 4 25
          THE METAPHORIC WOMB OF INTELLIGENCE

CHAPTER 5 35
          OPENING CLOSED METAPHORIC WOMBS

CHAPTER 6 45
          PRAYER TO OPEN CLOSED WOMB

CHAPTER 7 51
          WOMB QUOTES AND CREDITS

CHAPTER ONE

Thanksgiving, Praise, And Prayer

Acts 16:22-26

"Then the multitude rose together against them, and the magistrates tore off their clothes and commanded them to be beaten with rods. And when they had laid many stripes on them, they threw them into prison, commanding the jailer to keep them securely. He put them into the inner prison and fastened their feet in the stocks, having received such a charge. But at midnight, Paul and Silas were praying and singing hymns to God, and the prisoners listened to them. Suddenly there was a great earthquake so that the foundations of the prison were shaken, and immediately all the doors were opened, and everyone's chains were loosed."

PRAISE QUOTE

"Even if God never did another good thing in our lives, we could spend the rest of this life praising Him for what He has already done."
— **Dillon Burroughs,**

PRAYER OF PRAISE

When you give thanks to the Almighty God, He grants you access. **Psalm 100:4** *"Enter into His gates with thanksgiving....."*

When you pray, you tell God about your problems, and God may answer by sending divine help. And He will show you great and mighty things. **Jeremiah 33:3**says, *"Call **to** me, and I will answer **you and tell you great** and **mighty things....**"*

But when you praise God, you tell your problems that your God is greater than the problem. You are telling your problem who God is and what He can do about your situation.

In Acts16:22-24, when Paul and Silas were in prison, even if they wanted to fight, there was no way they could win because the forces against them were overwhelming. They were not only imprisoned but they were bound. Nevertheless, they walked out of jail without a fight. *What Did They Do To Get This Victory?*

All they did was praised, God. Therefore, like never before, go ahead and begin to praise The Almighty God! And you will be victorious without a fight. Praise Him with all your heart! Adore Him! Magnify and glorify His Holy Name! Honor Him with your praise! Lift Him high now! Exalt His Holy Name!

PRAISE JEHOVAH

O Lord, I bless Your Holy Name! Hallelujah! Eternal Rock of Ages, the Way the Truth and the Life, the Lion of the Tribe of Judah, the Lord of Host, the One who has never lost a battle, King of kings, Lord of Lords, the I am that I am. The Ancient of days, the Unchangeable Changer, the Unchangeable God glory be to Your holy Name. The Alpha and the Omega, the Beginning and the Ending, the One who was, the One who is, the One who is to come. The Almighty God, Jehovah El-Shaddai, Jehovah Shalom, The Prince of Peace, Jehovah Rapa, the great Physician, Jehovah Nissi, King of glory, glory be to Your Holy Name. You have the key of David; when You open, no man can shut when You close, no man can open. When You kill, no one can make alive; when You make alive, no man can kill. When You say yes, no man can say no, when You say no, no man can say yes, glory be to Your holy Name in Jesus Precious Name I worship Amen.

THANKSGIVING QUOTE

"Gratitude is the inward feeling of kindness received. Thankfulness is the natural impulse to express that feeling. Thanksgiving is the following of that impulse." — **Henry Van Dyke**

PRAYER OF THANKSGIVING

Psalm 100:4 *"Enter into His gates with thanksgiving, And into His courts with praise. Be thankful to Him, and bless His Name. Amen!*

Saint! Gratitude grants you greater access to more incredible blessings. Your attitude of gratitude is the determinant of your altitude in life. A grateful heart is a thankful heart. You can't be *'praise-full'* until you *are grateful,* and if you are not grateful, you cannot be joyful. When you are thankful, you always receive more.

APPRECIATE THE LORD

Go ahead now and thank God for what He did for you in the past so that He may do more today. *Lord Jesus, thank You for what You did for me yesterday, thank You for last week, thank You for the previous month, and thank You for years past.*

I thank You for healings and deliverance. Thank You for joy and the joy of salvation, thank You Lord for breakthroughs, miracles, signs, and wonders, and thank You for the salvation of souls.

I give You all the glory, all honor, and adoration for what You did in the past, for what You are doing, and what You will yet do. Thank you, Father, thank You Holy Spirit! Thank You, Lord Jesus. In Jesus Precious, I give thanks. Amen!

PRAYER OF PETITION AND SUPPLICATION

Philippians 4:6 "*Be anxious for nothing, but in everything by prayer and supplication, with thanksgiving, let your requests be made known to God.*"

SUPPLICATION QUOTE

When God is about to do great work, He pours out a spirit of supplication. - **Jonathan Edwards.**

PRAYER OF PETITION AND SUPPLICATION

PRAYER 1 - *Father, extraordinarily visit me today!*

PRAYER 2 - *Lord Jesus, every metaphorical womb the enemy has shut against me, thrust them open now!*

PRAYER 3 - *Holy Spirit, open the womb to my joy, to my success and progress in Jesus' Gracious Name. Amen!*

PRAYER 4 - *El-Shaddai permanently, shut the womb to sorrow and suffering in my life in Jesus' Name. Amen!*

PRAYER 5 - *Holy Father, let barrenness in any form send in my family now the Name Jesus Christ. Amen!*

PRAYER 6 - *Now, and ask God whatever you want Him to do for you today in Jesus' Mighty Name. Amen!*

Prayer 7 - *Thank the Lord in Advance for Hearing and Answering Your Prayers.*

CHAPTER TWO

DEFINITION OF TERM

QUOTE

"In asking forgiveness of women for our mythologizing of their bodies, for being unreal about them, we can only appeal to their sexuality, which is different but not different, perhaps, from our own. For women, too, there seems to be that tangle of supplication and possessiveness, that descent toward infantile undifferentiating, that omnipotent helplessness, that merger with the cosmic mother-warmth, that flushed pulse-quickened leap into

overestimation, projection, general mix-up."-**John Updike**

METAPHOR OF THE WOMB

Luke 5:2-7 *"...And he entered into one of the ships, which was Simon's, and prayed that he would thrust out a little from the land. And he sat down and taught the people out of the ship. When he had left speaking, he said unto Simon, Launch out into the deep, and let down your nets for a draught.*

And Simon answering said unto him, Master, we have toiled all the night and have taken nothing: nevertheless, I will let down the net at thy word. And when they had this done, they enclosed a great multitude of fishes: and their net brake. And they beckoned unto their partners, which were in the other ship, that they should come and help them. And they came and filled both the ships so that they began to sink."

WHAT IS METAPHOR?

A metaphor is a figure of speech in which a word or phrase is applied to an object or action to which it is not applicable. A metaphor is a thing regarded as representative or symbolic of something else, especially something abstract. Some synonyms of metaphor include a figure of speech, figurative expression, image, trope, allegory, parable and adages, analogy, symbol · emblem, story, tale, myth, legend, saga, fable, and apologue. Etc.

WHAT IS A WOMB?

Womb pronounced [wo͞om]. It is a noun. It is the organ in the lower body of a woman or female mammal where offspring are conceived and gestate before birth; the uterus.

A womb is where a seed develops. It's a place where the seed begins the journey to becoming a fruit. When the husband meets the wife, he drops a seed into the womb, and the embryo develops in the womb and comes forth as a fruit. **Psalm 127:3**says, "Children are the fruit of the womb."

THE SOIL IS A WOMB

The womb of the farmer is the ground. He plants a seed into the ground. The seed develops in the ground and produces something that will ultimately produce fruit for the farmer.

John 12:24 *says, "Except a grain of wheat falls to the ground and dies, it remains alone."*

So until you put the seed into the ground, it will remain alone, just a seed! But when it gets into the soil, into its womb, then it multiplies. That is why the fruitfulness of the farmer is determined by how good the ground is. The Bible says in **Matthew 13:23,** *"But he who received seed on the good ground is he who hears the word and understands it, who indeed bears fruit and* *produces: some a hundredfold, some sixty, some thirty."*

Some soil [womb] will produce 30-fold, some 60-fold, and some 100-fold. ***IT IS A METAPHOR!*** So, the womb of the fisherman is the river. The womb of the student is the brain. So, there are various kinds of metaphoric wombs.

QUOTE

"If you can't go back to your mother's womb, you'd better learn to be a good fighter."
— **Anchee Min, Red Azalea**

CHAPTER THREE

METAPHORIC WOMBS

Psalms 127:3 *"Lo, children are a heritage of the LORD: and the fruit of the **womb** is his reward."*

QUOTE

"You cannot choose the womb that houses you, but you can determine the tomb that takes you home." — Ikechukwu Izuakor

METAPHORIC WOMBS

When we talk about barrenness, we are not just about the woman trusting God for children; a student constantly failing his examinations is mentally barren. That means the brain, which is the womb of the student, is not producing results.

PROGRESS IS A WOMB

Progress has wombs. When God shuts the womb of progress, then no matter how hard you try, instead of moving forward, you'll be moving backward.

In the Book of **Jonah Chapters 1-4,** God sent Jonah to a particular place. Here is where I want you to go. Jonah and Jonah said no and went in the opposite direction, and they got into the ship and began to move. As God shut the womb of progress, it was going backward and downwards instead of going forward. When God closes the womb of progress, you will find that you are making all the effort to go forward, but rather, you will be going backward. But when He opens the womb of progress, suddenly you find that you'll take one tiny step, and you'll find yourself in a place you didn't even expect!

In **John 6:15-21,** the Bible tells us a story. The disciples were in a boat rowing very hard, and there was a storm, and because of the storm, instead of making progress, they were having problems. Suddenly, they saw Jesus walking towards them on the river, and they were afraid. And He said, don't be frightened, and they took Him into the boat. As soon as He stepped into the ship, the ship arrived at its destination instantly.

BLESSING IS A WOMB

Blessings have a womb. Scripturally, the Bible indicates that a womb can be shut. And it can be open. In **Genesis 48:17-19,** Jacob blessed the two sons of Joseph, and he gave the enormous blessing to Ephraim, the younger son. He placed the right hand on his head and the left hand on Manasseh. Within a short time, according to **Deuteronomy 3:17,** Ephraim had become ten times greater!

When God decides to open the womb of your blessings, it becomes gold when you

touch one little thing. You sell water and become a millionaire and build a house. It means God had opened the womb of your blessing. But God can shut the womb of blessings. When He does, things dry up.

Ephraim became ten times richer than his brother; after he became rich, He forgot God. God kept saying to him: Ephraim, we are friends, I love you, I did this for you, I did that for you, don't do this, don't do that.

Ephraim refused; he said, let me enjoy myself. Finally, in **Hosea 4:17,** God said Ephraim had joined himself to idols, leave him alone, and God said in **Hosea 5:9** He said Ephraim should be desolate. When I prospered you, you forgot me. I have the key; I can open, I can shut. *I pray that the* *blessing that is coming your way will not take you away from God. Amen!*

POVERTY IS A WOMB

Poverty has a womb. When God shuts the womb of poverty, you will discover that you will never lack again. God has a way of taking somebody beyond the boundary of poverty once and for all. In **2ⁿᵈKings 4:1-7,** there was a widow who had been in debt for as long as she can remember until her creditors said, if you don't pay by tomorrow, we will sell your children! She cried to God. God turned the tide, and she never borrowed again.

Wealth has a womb. When God opens the womb of wealth, all of a sudden, poverty becomes a stranger. In **Exodus 12:35-36,** the children of Israel who had been in poverty for more than 430 years became wealthy in one single night. It took God only one night. *I prophesy your night is now in Jesus' Name!*

BREAKTHROUGH IS A WOMB

Breakthroughs have a womb. When God opens the womb of victories, one breakthrough will begin to follow another. In the story of Peter in **Luke 5:1-11,** Peter had one breakthrough that he caught a lot of fish, but other breakthroughs followed. He was promoted from fisherman to fisher of men. He moved from there and preached one sermon and won 3,000 souls. He preached another sermon; 5,000 souls won. He preached another one multitudes came! *I prophesy even as you are celebrating one breakthrough, two others will follow quickly in Jesus' Name. Amen!*

QUOTE

"You were born a winner, a warrior, one who defied the odds by surviving the most gruesome battle of them all - the race to the egg. And now that you are a giant, why do you even doubt victory against smaller numbers and wider margins? The only walls that exist are those you have placed in your mind. And whatever obstacles you conceive exist only because you have forgotten what you have already achieved." — **Suzy Kassem**

CHAPTER FOUR

THE METAPHORIC WOMB OF INTELLIGENCE

Ecclesiastes 7:7 *"Surely oppression maketh a wise man mad; and a gift destroyeth the heart."*

QUOTE

"A genius is produced not by a woman's womb but by a man's efforts."
— Mokokoma Mokhonoana

Metaphorically speaking, intelligence has a womb. When the Almighty God opens your womb of wisdom, knowledge, and understanding, you become so clever people cannot understand how come. In **2ndChronicles 1:6-12,** when Solomon asked for wisdom, knowledge, and understanding from God and God released it unto him, King Solomon became the wisest man who ever lived. *As many students read this, I prophesy that now God shall open the womb of wisdom, knowledge, and understanding unto you in Jesus' Name. Amen!*

Some people read the same thing you are reading, and by the time they've read it once or twice, they've got it all. When we were in school, we used to say that such people have a photographic brain. If people can have a photographic brain, you also can be one of them. And it is all in God's hands. *I decree in the Mighty Name of Jesus Christ; you will never fail another examination in Jesus' Name. Amen!*

And when God shuts your womb of wisdom, knowledge, and understanding, people you think should be quick and intelligent begin to do foolish and stupid things. In **Exodus 14:21-23,** the Bible says Moses raised his hand, the Red Sea opened, and the children of Israel went across the sea on dry land. And the Egyptians followed. Think about it!

You are pursuing a people, and their God opened a door in the belly of the sea? Any intelligent person will say I must not go further. But God locked the womb of their intelligence. That's why they followed! *I decree that every enemy pursuing you and your loved ones shall drown this time in the Name of Jesus Christ, our Lord, and Savior. Amen!*

OPPORTUNITY IS A METAPHORICAL WOMB

An opportunity has a womb. When God opens the possibility, you discover chance coming from the right, left, and center! In **1stKings 17:8-16,** a widow was gathering sticks to prepare the last meal when suddenly an opportunity came, and the Man of God said to her, give me the food first, then after that, you can prepare your own. It was the opportunity of a lifetime.

The woman grabbed it, and there was enough food for her, her son, throughout the famine. Opportunities happen when God opens the womb of possibility. *The Almighty God shall open the womb of opportunities to you from today in the Name of Jesus Christ. Amen!*

When the door of opportunity is shut, problems follow. *I pray that from today, the womb of opportunity will be open unto you in Jesus' Name. Amen!*

ANOINTING IS A METAPHORICAL WOMB

I can categorically declare that The Anointing of the Holy Ghost has a metaphoric womb. When God opens the womb of anointing, your body will be carrying high voltage, divine electricity.

In **Judges 15:14,** the Bible says Samson was bound and brought before his enemies, but the womb of anointing was opened. The Bible said the Spirit of God came down mightily upon him, and the rope that bound him to cut itself as if it were something that caught fire.

Many years ago, when I was younger, I didn't have as much wisdom as I have now. I was coming down from the mountain, and I went to see a friend of mine. He was not expecting me, but he came out and invited me in when he heard the car. As the man tried to embrace me, the anointing hit him like a thunderbolt, and he collapsed on the floor because of the slaying anointing upon my life. Now! that's the anointing

I tell you! There is something called anointing, the real thing, the original One, the real McCoy; it will begin to operate in your life from now in Jesus' Name!

What happened to the anointing? You may ask! *It's still there. It's just that now we know how to control it. That day the womb of anointing was opened. But at that time, I didn't know how to handle it, but that anointing is still there. It's only that we know how to control it now.*

THE METAPHORIC WOMB OF DEATH

Death has a womb. When God shut the womb of death, there will be no burial. In

Mark 5:35-44, Jarius' daughter was dead, but she couldn't be buried because Jesus took her by the hand and said, *little girl, I say to you, arise!* And death couldn't swallow her.

In **Luke 7:11-15,** a widow was going to bury her only son. Jesus met her on the way! And said, no, don't go! The young man - come back! *If the enemy had decided to kill you or your loved ones, by the power of God, I shut the womb of death in Jesus' Name! Amen!*

I decree in the Name of the One called the Resurrection, and the life, the womb of death against you is shut in Jesus' Name!

I pray that the death plan of the enemy for you and your loved ones is canceled in Jesus' Name.

You shall live and not die to give glory to God! Amen!

When the Almighty God decided to open the womb of the grave, even the grave births the living; when the Lord first stood by the graveyard of Lazarus and said Lazarus, come forth! Lazarus, who had been in the womb of the grave for four days, came out alive. When God opens the womb of a woman, babies begin to jump out. **1ˢᵗSamuel 2:21,** after God opened the womb of Hannah with Samuel, five others followed! *For you that the world has been calling you barren because of the One who lives forever, soon and very soon* *they'll be counting your children in Jesus' Name!*

Death is a symbolic womb. It can be shut and opened!

QUOTE

"Wonder begins in the womb of a woman."
— Lailah Gifty Akita

CHAPTER 5

OPENING CLOSED METAPHORIC WOMBS

Isaiah 44:24 *"Thus saith the LORD, thy redeemer, and he that formed thee from the **womb**, I am the LORD that maketh all things; that stretcheth forth the heavens alone; that spreadeth abroad the earth by myself."*

QUOTE

"Sensuality is the womb of creation."
— Lebo Grand

OPENING CLOSED METAPHORIC WOMBS

Now the question to answer is how can we a shut metaphoric womb open? What do I do so that God can open the door of fruitfulness unto me?

DIVINE VISITATION

Please note the following. Without divine visitation, there cannot be divine intervention. And without divine intervention, there will never be a divine manifestation of your expectation. Open the door to fruitfulness begins with divine visitation. To open a door, the One who has the key must come.

In Luke 5, Jesus went to the Lake of Gennesaret. He arrived there to visit Peter. ***The Almighty God will visit you today in Jesus' Name!***

PRAISE

Praise is the catalyst for the divine presence. For God inhabits the praises of His people. Psalm 22:3 When you praise Him, He comes to you. **John 4:24-25** says He's seeking for those who will worship Him, so when He finds a worshipper, He visits. The door to open womb begins by divine visitation but triggered praise.

DIVINE CHOICE

So, Open doors to breakthrough begin by divine visitation followed by divine choice. God chose the boat of Peter. ***May He*** *choose your boat today in Jesus' Name. Amen!*

CHOICE BY HIS MERCY

Because He said, I will be merciful unto whom I will be merciful; *He will be merciful to you tonight.*

And then, when we talk about Peter surrendering His boat, the boat did not belong to Peter; the ship belonged to God. The Bible says the earth is the Lord's and the fullness thereof. Your body belongs to God; your womb belongs to God. So, don't deny Him of what belongs to Him.

The Bible says your body is the temple of the Holy Spirit. Don't use, misuse and abuse that body. You want Him to give you babies, but God says stop committing adultery and fornication. Your body must be kept holy; it must be kept as a living sacrifice to the Almighty God.

FAITHFULNESS IN TITHE AND OFFERING

Do you want God to open the womb of blessing? Don't forget to rob Him of His tithe. He said that if you bring all the tithes into His house, He will open the windows of heaven and pour in a blessing. He will open the womb of blessing and pour out blessing unto you that there will not be enough room to receive it. If you fail to tithe, everything will be financially tight for you.

FIRST FRUIT

Don't rob Him of His first fruits because He said in **Proverbs 3:9-10** if you honor Him with your first fruit, He said He would look upon the womb of blessing. He told your storehouse will burst.

SERVE HIM

What must I do so that God will open the womb of blessing? Serve Him until He says thank you! That's what He did for Peter He said, I need your boat. Peter said you are welcome, sir!

He said, push away from the land. Yes, Lord. And He sat down in the boat and began to preach. Peter stood there, patiently, until He finished His preaching, and then He now said, I decide to say thank you. Launch into the deep, throw your nets to the right.

God knows where your fish are gathered. He knows where your breakthroughs are. He knows how many children He can give you. He has millions of them. He is the owner of silver and gold! There's nothing that you can ask for that is too much for Jehovah!

DILIGENCE

Follow Jesus diligently. If Peter had not followed Jesus, he would have had only one breakthrough, but when he got to land, he forsook all and followed Jesus. That's why he moved from one breakthrough to another; Follow Jesus diligently.

Some of us, once we get a miracle from God we disappear. What He has given you is just the first. There is more to come. Stay with Him!

SALVATION IS NEEDED

If you have not surrendered your life to this Jesus, do it now. Let Him save your soul. Let Him bring about a change in you. Let Him open the door of salvation to you, and everything will change for good for you. This is your hour of salvation, the gates of mercy are open now; the womb of salvation is available now. The moment your sins are gone, your breakthrough can come.

He wants to be merciful unto you. *Say! Lord Jesus! Forgive all my sins, and I will* *serve you for the rest of my life, and I will follow you all of the ways! Just have mercy on me! Save my soul!*

Ask that the Almighty God have mercy on you! *Say Have an understanding on me, O Lord! Forgive all my sins, and I will follow You all the days of my life. Thank You, Jesus! In Jesus' mighty Name, I have prayed!*

Eternal Rock of Ages, I bless Your Holy Name for Your Word that has gone forth today. Please Almighty God have mercy on us in Jesus' Name! Receive us in Jesus' Name! Forgive us in Jesus' Name! Wipe away all our sins with Your Blood in Jesus' Name! Write our names in the Book of Life in Jesus' Name! Beginning from now, let everything become new for us in Jesus'

Name! Thank You, my Father, in Jesus' Mighty Name I have prayed!

CHAPTER SIX

PRAYER TO OPEN CLOSED WOMB

*"He maketh the barren woman to keep house and to be a joyful mother of children. Praise ye the LORD. "***Psalm 113:9**

QUOTE

"We know from the lives of the saints and Holy Scripture that from their mother's womb, children can sense the presence of God."

— Sister Magdalen

PRAYER TO OPEN CLOSED WOMB

Hallelujah! Amen! I am confident God wants you to remember today for the rest of your life. So, you bless the Name of the Lord. Your day has come!

Hannah's day came. It was because she was praying as she had never prayed before. There are prayers you pray as if to say to God, well if You answer, OK if You don't reply, fine! But there are some prayers that you pray that God Himself will hear and say I must answer this fellow! You want to pray the kind of prayer that will move the heavens for a few minutes because I know that you are tired of barrenness, whether physical, material, or spiritual.

I know I am tired of poverty; I am tired of failure! I am tired of defeat. I don't want to weep anymore.

If you are determined that today something must happen, then you must pray until something happens—[PUSH].

I call this prayer the labor room prayer. Pray the kind of prayer that a woman will pray in the labor room. There they don't pray like ladies and gentlemen. They pray in such a way that everybody will know they are praying.

God can do anything that He wants to do today. When the mother of Jesus came to Him in the wedding in Cana of Galilee in **John 2,** they said they had no wine; Jesus said, woman, why are you bothering me? It is not my time. But that day, the time came. The time is coming for someone here tonight. I want us to pray these prayers for a few minutes! I want you to stand on your feet.

PRAYERS TO OPEN METAPHORIC WOMB

PRAYER 1 *Lord, open the womb of miracles to me today! Call on the Almighty God! Father, Pastor Stevie is calling on you today; open the womb of miracles unto me now! Lord, open the womb of miracles! Signs and wonders for me today in Jesus' Mighty Name, I pray! Amen!*

PRAYER 2 *Success has its womb, a breakthrough has its womb, and progress has its womb; talk to God and says, Lord Jesus! Open the womb of success and progress to me! Open the womb of breakthroughs to me! Go ahead! Lord, You have the key of David! Open the* *womb of breakthrough! The womb of victory unto me today in Jesus' Precious Name I prayed! Amen!*

PRAYER 3 *Holy Father, I know You cannot fail! Don't let my own be impossible with you in Jesus' Name. Amen!*

PRAYER 4 *You know the areas where you are barren; maybe it is health or the area of poverty or lack of promotion or failure in examination or failure in life or lack of a future partner. Go to God now, Say I have prayed before, but now this is different, answer me today, Lord! This One is different, O Lord! Have mercy on me? Let today be my turning point! Help me, Lord! I have nowhere else to go; why should the world say where my God is?*

PRAYER 5 *Father, I bless Your Holy Name because I know You can't fail. Accept my thanks in Jesus' Name!*

a. *Father, every sin that stands between me and my miracle, forgive me today in Jesus' Name!*

b. *Lord, today open the doors or womb of blessing to me.*

c. *Open the womb of all the barren in Jesus' Name!*

d. *Open the womb of fruitfulness to them in Jesus' Name!*

e. *Open the womb of wealth to them in Jesus' Name!*

f. *Open the womb of progress to them in Jesus' Name!*

g. *Open the womb of breakthrough to us in Jesus' Name!*

h. *Open the womb of anointing to us in Jesus' Name!*

i. *Lord! I know You can't fail, so help me succeed!*

j. *Thank You, Father, in Jesus' Name, I have prayed!*

CHAPTER SEVEN

WOMB QUOTES AND CREDITS

1. *"If you can't go back to your mother's womb, you'd better learn to be a good fighter."*
   — Anchee Min, Red Azalea

2. *"You were born a winner, a warrior, one who defied the odds by surviving the most gruesome battle of them all - the race to the egg. And now that you are a giant, why do you even doubt victory against smaller numbers*

and wider margins? The only walls that exist are those you have placed in your mind. And whatever obstacles you conceive, exist only because you have forgotten what you have already achieved."— Suzy Kassem,

3. *"Bless your mum, who carried you for nine months in her womb."*— Lailah Gifty Akita

4. *"The wonder of life begins in the womb of a woman."*— Lailah Gifty Akita

5. *"You cannot choose the womb that houses you, but you can determine the tomb that takes you home."*— Ikechukwu Izuakor

6. *"A genius is produced not by a woman's womb but by a man's efforts.*— Mokokoma Mokhonoana

7. *"We all come out of the womb needing love to grow and develop properly."* — Ken Poirot

8. *"A woman is a pure and immaculate sentence, a linguistic proposition that even if you remove the proper punctuation, she still stands as an elegant independent sentence, the only sentence that subverts all linguistic and grammatical rules. She does not need a male signifier or qualifier to positively assert her value and meaning because her being, sui generis, is already*

intrinsically defined by her "womb," the quintessence of her femininity, synonymous with the birthing and the nurturing of humanity. And for that, regardless of who she is, she epitomizes Grace, Truth, Goodness, and Beauty, a précis of her ontological linguistic presence, as a sublime perfect sentence. — Danny Castillones Sillada

9. *"Never you look down on your Abraham because of your Sarah because the blessing is not in the womb of Sarah but the loins of Abraham."*— Ikechukwu Izuakor

10. *"Mary considers how the womb stirs and years for its children, even after they have grown and gone off to other lives. The womb*

remembers. The womb knows how to weep."
— Walter Wangerin Jr.

11. *"Hello world, goodbye womb."*— Steven Magee

12. *"The wonder of the womb is the birth of a child."*— Lailah Gifty Akita

13. *"What is the measure of life but the distance traveled from womb to catacomb, does the ever after take account?"*— Phen Weston

14. *"Leaving Wychwood gave him, as it did each time, the mingled anxiety and exhilaration of a rebirth. Womb-warm and sequestered, It was at once a sanctuary and a place of*

internment." — Lucy Hughes-Hallett

15. *"We know from the lives of the saints and Holy Scripture that from their mother's womb, children can sense the presence of God."*
— Sister Magdalen

16. *"Wonder originates in the womb of a woman."*
— Lailah Gifty Akita

17. *"The greatest of all wonders is conception in the womb of a woman."* — Lailah Gifty Akita

18. *"Wonder begins in the womb of a woman."*
— *Lailah Gifty Akita*

19. *"Who can understand how a child is formed in a womb of a woman?"*— Lailah Gifty Akita

20. *"Sensuality is the womb of creation.*
    — Lebo Grand

21. *"Who can understand how life begins in the womb of a woman?"*— Lailah Gifty Akita

22. *"According to the Scriptures, there is a promise of children for the barren womb in the sacred time."*— Lailah Gifty Akita

23. *"Joseph is an example of true patience and endurance in the plan of God. From the moment we are conceived in the womb, our*

destiny is being shaped by God the Father. From the life of Joseph, we can learn what it is to suffer for God, what it is to truly die to self and the blessing that God bestows upon those who lay down their lives in service to Him and the resurrection power of new beginnings that only God can bring to pass by and through His Spirit of grace." — Paddick Van Zyl

BIBLE VERSES ON WOMB

- *"He maketh the barren woman to keep house and to be a joyful mother of children. Praise ye the LORD."* Psalm 113:9

- **Jeremiah 1:5** *"Before I formed you in **the womb** I knew you, before* *you were born I set you apart; I appointed you as **a** prophet to the nations."*

- **Psalm 22:9-11** *"Yet you brought me out of **the** womb; you made me trust in you, even at my mother's breast. I was cast on you; from my mother's **womb,** you have been my God. Do is not far from me, for trouble is near, and there is no one to help."*
- **Isaiah 66:7-9** *"Before she goes into labor, she gives birth; before **the** pains come upon her, she delivers a son. Who has ever heard **of** such things? Who has ever seen things like this? Can a country be born in a day, or a nation be brought forth in **a** moment? Yet no sooner is Zion in labor than she gives birth to her children. Do I bring to the moment of birth and not give delivery?"*

says the LORD. "Do I close up the womb when I bring to delivery?" says your God."

- **Isaiah 49:5** *"And now the LORD says- he who formed me in **the womb** to be his servant to bring Jacob back to him and gather Israel to himself, for I am honored in the eyes of the LORD and my God has been my strength."*
- **Isaiah 44:2** *"This is what the LORD says- he who made you, who formed you in **the womb**, and who will help you: Do not be afraid, Jacob, my servant, Jeshurun, whom I have chosen."*
- **Job 31:15** *"Did not he who made me in **the womb** make them? Did not the same One form us both within our mothers?"*

- **Psalm 139:13** *"For you created my inmost being; you knit me together in my mother's **womb**."*

BLESS THE NAME OF OUR LORD JESUS CHRIST.

Other Books by Apostle Stevie Okauru

The Christ we Eat
The Oracle decoding dream
The Oracle DIY Deliverance Kit
Effectual Fasting Kit
Miracle sermon note

Available on Amazon.com or Barnes & Nobles and other major books stores all over the world.

www.ingramcontent.com/pod-product-compliance
Lightning Source LLC
LaVergne TN
LVHW042000060526
838200LV00041B/1801